THE INCREDIBLE
WORLD
OF WONDERS

SCIENCE, ANIMALS, EARTH, AND BEYOND

COPYRIGHT

All content within this *The Incredible World of Wonders* including texts, templates, and designs, is protected by copyright. The intellectual property rights belong to us and may not be reproduced, duplicated, or used in any form without our explicit permission.

DISCLAIMER

The information and guidance provided in this book are for general purposes only. We make no representations or warranties of any kind, express or implied, about the completeness, accuracy, reliability, suitability, or availability of the information contained herein. Any reliance you place on such information is therefore strictly at your own risk.

While we strive to provide accurate and up-to-date content, we do not guarantee the accuracy or effectiveness of the techniques, strategies, or advice presented in this journal. We shall not be held liable for any errors, omissions, or damages arising from the use of this book or the information it contains.

It is important to note that this book is not a substitute for professional advice or assistance. If you require specific guidance or have any concerns, we recommend consulting a qualified professional.

By using this *The Incredible World of Wonders*, you acknowledge and accept the terms of this Copyright & Disclaimer statement.

Table of Contents

	PAGES
Introduction	4 - 5
Chapter 1: Amazing Animals	6 - 13
Animal Facts	6 - 13
Chapter 2: Science Spectacles	14 - 31
Experiments	14 - 21
Science Fun Facts	22 - 31
Chapter 3: Earth's Wonders	32 - 77
Natural Marvels	32 - 39
Weather Wonders	40 - 46
Ecosystems in Harmony	47 - 53
Earth's Mysteries	54 - 61
Earth's Landmarks	62 - 69
Earth Illustrations	70 - 77
Chapter 4: Everything in Between	78-93
Microscopic Marvels	78 - 85
Microorganisms and Beyond	86 - 93
Chapter 5: Beyond Our World	94 - 117
Space Facts	94 - 101
Astronaut Adventures	102 - 109
Space Illustrations	110 - 117

THE INCREDIBLE WORLD OF WONDERS:
SCIENCE, ANIMALS, EARTH, AND BEYOND

Are you ready to embark on an extraordinary adventure like no other? Great! Let's begin by opening the door to a world filled with awe, wonder, and endless possibilities.

Imagine a world where giraffes touch the sky with their long necks, cheetahs race at lightning speed, and chameleons perform color-changing magic tricks. Picture a world where the Earth's landscapes hold secrets waiting to be uncovered, where the universe stretches out into the cosmos, inviting us to explore its mysteries.

This book is your passport to that world—a world where science unlocks the secrets of the smallest particles and the vastness of space, where animals reveal their incredible abilities and quirks, and where the Earth itself showcases its breathtaking beauty and power.

But here's the best part: YOU are the explorer, the scientist, the adventurer. With each turn of the page, you'll dive into new realms of knowledge and imagination. You'll discover how our planet's landscapes were shaped, how animals have adapted to thrive in their environments, and how the universe dances with stars, planets, and galaxies.

Throughout your journey, you'll encounter fascinating facts, captivating illustrations, and interactive surprises that make learning an exhilarating experience. So, don't just read this book—immerse yourself in it! Ask questions, seek answers, and let your curiosity lead the way.

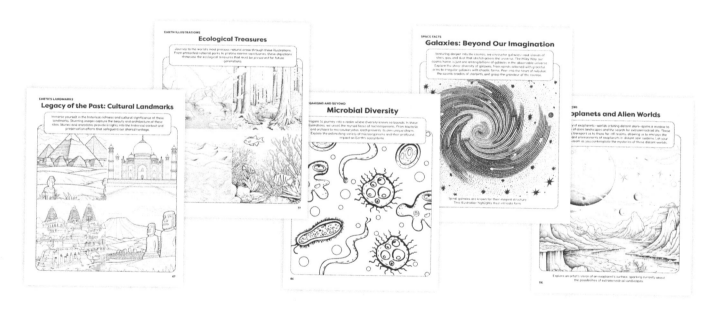

The Incredible World of Wonders is more than just a book; it's a gateway to understanding, a spark for your imagination, and an invitation to join the ranks of young explorers who are eager to uncover the mysteries of our incredible world.

Are you ready to dive in? Turn the page, and let the adventure begin!

Giraffes

Giraffes are Tall Giants

Giraffes are famous for their incredibly long necks, which can reach heights as tall as two grown-up humans stacked on top of each other! This unique feature allows them to reach tasty leaves high up in the trees that other animals can't access.

Spots and Patterns

Each giraffe's coat is adorned with a beautiful pattern of spots, which are like their fingerprints—no two giraffes have the same pattern.

Fun Fact:

A giraffe's tongue is purple! It helps them pluck leaves from thorny branches without getting hurt.

Cheetahs

Speedy Sprinters
Cheetahs are the fastest land animals on Earth! They can sprint at incredible speeds of up to 60 miles per hour (97 kilometers per hour).

Distinctive Spots
Cheetahs are known for their beautiful spotted coats, which help them blend into the grasslands when they're hunting for prey.

Sprint and Rest
After a high-speed chase to catch their prey, cheetahs need some time to recover, as they get tired quickly.

Chameleons

Curious Tongues

Chameleons have long, sticky tongues that shoot out lightning-fast to catch insects. It's like having a built-in insect-catching tool!

Masters of Camouflage

Chameleons are experts at changing the color and texture of their skin to blend in with their surroundings. They use this amazing skill to hide from predators and catch insects.

Fun Fact: Chameleons can change colors to express their emotions, like excitement or calmness.

Swiveling Eyes

Chameleons have the incredible ability to move their eyes in different directions independently, which means they can look in two places at once!

Dolphins

Smart and Social
Dolphins are some of the smartest and most sociable animals in the ocean. They communicate with each other using clicks, whistles, and body language.

Fun Fact: Each dolphin has its own unique whistle, like a personal name!

Acrobatic Swimmers
Dolphins love to leap out of the water, ride the waves created by boats, and even surf. They are the acrobats of the sea!

Playful Personalities
Dolphins have playful and curious natures, which makes them a favorite among ocean lovers.

Penguins

Penguin Parade
Penguins are social birds that live in large groups called colonies. They often gather on the icy shores of Antarctica and march together in what looks like a fun parade.

Flippers and Swimmers
Penguins are excellent swimmers. Their flippers help them navigate through the water with ease. Some penguins can even leap out of the water and onto the ice with a big splash!

Cold-Resistant Feathers
Penguins have thick layers of feathers that keep them warm in icy waters. These feathers are waterproof, which means penguins stay dry even while swimming.

Octopuses

Incredible Intelligence
Octopuses are some of the smartest creatures in the ocean. They can solve puzzles, open jars, and even find their way through mazes. They're like the Einstein of the sea!

Masters of Disguise
Octopuses are experts at camouflage. They can change the color and texture of their skin to blend in with their surroundings. It's like having an invisibility cloak!

Eight Is Great
Octopuses have eight long, flexible arms covered in suckers. These arms help them catch prey, explore their environment, and even communicate with other octopuses.

Elephants

Gentle Giants

Elephants are the largest land animals on Earth. Despite their size, they are known for their gentle and caring nature. They form close-knit family groups called herds.

Social Bonds

Elephants are highly social animals and have deep emotional bonds within their herds. They show affection by touching and hugging each other with their trunks.

Trunk Tricks

An elephant's trunk is an incredible tool. It can pick up heavy objects, spray water, and even sense vibrations in the ground, helping them communicate with other elephants far away.

Butterflies

Metamorphosis Magic

Butterflies go through a magical transformation called metamorphosis. They start as tiny eggs, hatch into caterpillars, form a chrysalis, and finally emerge as colorful butterflies.

Long-Distance Flyers

Some butterflies are great travelers. They migrate thousands of miles to find warmer climates or better food sources. It's like going on a butterfly adventure!

Colorful Wings

Butterflies have intricate patterns and vibrant colors on their wings. These beautiful designs help them attract mates and sometimes even scare away predators.

Colorful Milk

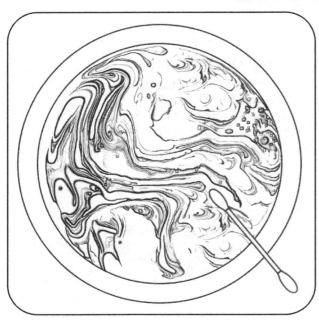

 **OBJECTIVE**

To demonstrate the effects of surface tension and the interaction of molecules in a fun and colorful way.

MATERIALS NEEDED:

- A shallow dish or plate
- Whole milk (a small amount)
- Liquid food coloring (different colors)
- Dishwashing liquid (a small amount)
- A cotton swab or toothpick
- Paper towels for cleanup

 PROCEDURE:

1. Pour a small amount of whole milk into the shallow dish or plate, just enough to cover the bottom.
2. Add a few drops of different liquid food coloring to the milk. Place the drops in various locations in the milk but not too close together.
3. Dip the cotton swab or toothpick into a tiny amount of dishwashing liquid.
4. Gently touch the milk surface with the soapy cotton swab or toothpick, right in the center of one of the food coloring drops.
5. Observe what happens as the colors begin to swirl and mix.

EXPLANATION:

This experiment demonstrates the principles of surface tension and the interaction of molecules. The milk's surface tension prevents the food coloring from immediately spreading out, but when the dish soap is added, it disrupts the surface tension and causes the colors to mix and move.

This experiment is both visually captivating and educational, making it a great choice for young readers. It encourages them to explore scientific concepts related to liquids, surface tension, and molecular interactions in a fun and memorable way.

Additionally, you can include safety tips and guidelines, such as adult supervision, when conducting experiments at home or in the classroom.

DIY Volcano

 OBJECTIVE

To create a miniature volcano that erupts with a bubbly, fizzy lava flow, demonstrating the principles of chemical reactions.

MATERIALS NEEDED:

- An empty plastic bottle (such as a small water or soda bottle)
- Baking soda
- Vinegar
- Dishwashing liquid
- Red food coloring
- Cardstock or construction paper
- Tape
- A small tray or dish to contain the eruption
- Optional: Clay or modeling dough for creating a volcano shape around the bottle

PROCEDURE:

1. Optional: If you'd like to create a volcano shape around the bottle, mold clay or modeling dough into a volcano cone shape, leaving the bottle's top open. Ensure that the bottle is securely placed in the center of the cone.
2. Place the bottle on the tray or dish.
3. In the empty bottle, add about two tablespoons of baking soda.
4. Add a few drops of red food coloring into the bottle.
5. Squirt a small amount of dishwashing liquid (just a drop or two) into the bottle.
6. Now, it's time to make the volcano erupt! Pour vinegar into the bottle, and watch as the chemical reaction occurs. You'll see a bubbly, fizzy eruption that looks like lava flowing down the volcano.

 EXPLANATION:

This experiment showcases a simple chemical reaction between the baking soda (a base) and vinegar (an acid). When combined, they react to produce carbon dioxide gas, which creates the fizzy eruption. The red food coloring and dishwashing liquid enhance the visual effect, making it resemble lava.

Be sure to include safety precautions, such as using a tray or dish to contain any spills, and conducting the experiment in a well-ventilated area.

Balloon Rocket

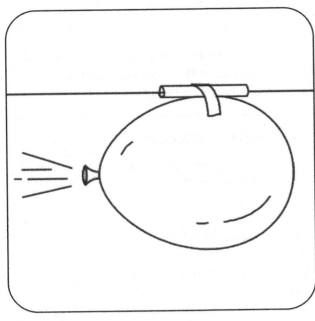

 OBJECTIVE

To demonstrate the principles of motion and propulsion using a simple balloon-powered rocket.

MATERIALS NEEDED:

- A long piece of string (about 10 feet or more)
- A drinking straw
- Tape
- A balloon
- Scissors
- Optional: Markers or stickers for decorating the balloon

PROCEDURE:

1. Decorate your balloon if you'd like. You can use markers or stickers to give it a personalized touch.
2. Cut the drinking straw in half and tape one end of the straw to the opening of the balloon. Make sure it's securely attached.
3. Thread the string through the straw, leaving a length of string on either side.
4. Stretch the string across a room or outdoor area, making sure it's taut and secured at both ends. The string should be at a slight incline, so the balloon can move along it.
5. Blow up the balloon and pinch the end to keep the air in.
6. Release the pinched end of the balloon, and watch as the air rushes out, propelling the balloon rocket along the string.

EXPLANATION:

This experiment demonstrates Newton's Third Law of Motion: "For every action, there is an equal and opposite reaction." When you release the pinched end of the balloon, the air escaping from the balloon in one direction creates an equal and opposite force in the other direction, propelling the balloon rocket along the string.

The balloon rocket experiment is not only entertaining but also provides a hands-on lesson in the fundamental principles of physics. It's a great way to introduce young readers to concepts of motion and forces while having a blast with a DIY rocket.

Include safety reminders, such as ensuring there are no obstacles or hazards in the path of the balloon rocket, and that the experiment is conducted in a safe and supervised environment.

Floating Egg

 **OBJECTIVE**

To demonstrate the concept of density and buoyancy by making an egg float in a glass of water.

MATERIALS NEEDED:

- A clear glass or container
- Water
- An egg

 PROCEDURE:

1. Fill the clear glass or container with water about three-fourths full.
2. Carefully place the egg into the glass of water.
3. Observe what happens to the egg. Does it sink to the bottom or float?
4. If the egg sinks, try gently adding salt to the water while stirring until the egg starts to float. Continue to add salt and stir until the egg remains suspended in the water.

 EXPLANATION:

This experiment illustrates the principles of density and buoyancy. When the egg is placed in plain water, it may initially sink because it is denser than the water. However, by adding salt to the water, you increase its density. Eventually, the water becomes denser than the egg, causing the egg to float due to buoyant force.

The Floating Egg experiment provides an engaging way for young readers to explore the concepts of density and buoyancy in a hands-on manner. It helps them understand why some objects float while others sink and introduces them to the idea of manipulating the density of liquids to achieve different outcomes.

Include safety guidelines, such as handling the egg with care and ensuring that any spilled water or salt is cleaned up promptly.

Rainbow in a Jar

 **OBJECTIVE**

To create a colorful and visually stunning rainbow in a jar, demonstrating the principles of density and liquid layering.

MATERIALS NEEDED:

- A tall, clear glass jar or vase
- Light corn syrup
- Dishwashing liquid
- Vegetable oil
- Water
- Food coloring (various colors)
- A dropper or pipette
- A small funnel (optional)

PROCEDURE:

1. Fill the glass jar or vase about one-third full with light corn syrup. This will be the first layer.
2. Carefully add an equal amount of dishwashing liquid to the jar using a dropper or pipette. Let it settle on top of the corn syrup as a separate layer.
3. Next, add an equal amount of vegetable oil to the jar. The oil will form another distinct layer.
4. Slowly add water to the jar, using the dropper or pipette to create a layer on top of the oil.
5. Now, for the fun part! Add a few drops of different food coloring to the water layer. Watch as the food coloring slowly descends through the water, creating colorful streaks.
6. Continue adding food coloring drops until you've created a beautiful rainbow of colors in the jar.
7. Observe the distinct layers of corn syrup, dishwashing liquid, oil, water, and the colorful rainbow. Each layer has a different density, which causes them to separate.

 EXPLANATION:

This experiment demonstrates the concept of density and liquid layering. Different liquids have different densities, and denser liquids sink below less dense ones. The food coloring provides a visual representation of this principle as it moves through the water layer.

The Rainbow in a Jar experiment not only introduces young readers to the concept of density but also offers a visually captivating experience. It's a fantastic way to learn about the properties of liquids and how they interact in a fun and colorful way.

Include safety instructions, such as handling food coloring with care and avoiding spills, to ensure a safe and enjoyable experiment.

Growing Crystal Geodes

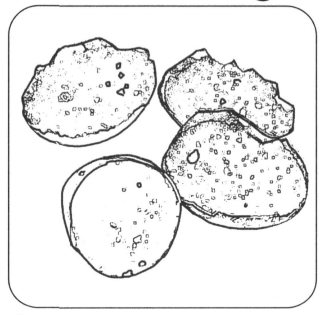

 OBJECTIVE

To create beautiful crystal geodes using simple household materials, demonstrating the process of crystal formation and saturation.

MATERIALS NEEDED:

- Clean eggshells (halves)
- Alum powder (readily available at most grocery stores)
- Hot water
- String or fishing line
- Popsicle sticks or clothespins
- A tall, clear glass or container
- Optional: Food coloring for colorful crystals

 PROCEDURE:

1. Carefully clean and dry the eggshells, and then cut them in half. You should have empty, clean eggshell halves.
2. Prepare a saturated alum solution by mixing hot water with alum powder. Stir until no more alum will dissolve. You can add a few drops of food coloring to create colorful crystals if desired.
3. Tie a piece of string or fishing line around the midpoint of a popsicle stick or clothespin.
4. Dip the eggshell halves into the alum solution, ensuring they are completely submerged. Let them soak for a minute or two.
5. Carefully remove the eggshells from the solution and allow them to dry for a little while. Then, hang the eggshells by the string or fishing line inside the tall glass or container so that they are partially immersed in the alum solution.
6. Place the glass or container in a location where it won't be disturbed. Over the next few days, you'll see beautiful crystal formations grow inside the eggshells.

EXPLANATION:

This experiment demonstrates the process of crystal formation through a process called crystallization. As the alum solution cools and evaporates, alum crystals form on the surface of the eggshells. The string or fishing line acts as a surface for crystal growth.

Growing Crystal Geodes is a visually stunning experiment that allows young readers to witness the fascinating process of crystal growth. It introduces them to concepts of saturation, crystallization, and the formation of beautiful natural structures.

Include safety tips, such as handling hot water with care and adult supervision when using alum powder.

Homemade Lava Lamp

 **OBJECTIVE**

To create a mesmerizing homemade lava lamp that demonstrates the interaction between water and oil, as well as the concept of density.

MATERIALS NEEDED:

- A clear plastic or glass bottle with a screw-on cap
- Water
- Vegetable oil
- Alka-Seltzer tablets (or similar effervescent tablets)
- Food coloring (optional)
- A flashlight or desk lamp (optional, for enhanced visual effect)

 PROCEDURE:

1. Fill the clear bottle about one-third full with water.
2. Carefully pour vegetable oil into the bottle until it's nearly full, leaving some space at the top.
3. If desired, add a few drops of food coloring to the oil. This will create colorful blobs in your "lava lamp."
4. Break an Alka-Seltzer tablet into smaller pieces.
5. Drop one small piece of the Alka-Seltzer tablet into the bottle and screw on the cap.
6. Observe as the tablet reacts with the water, creating bubbles that rise to the top of the oil. This mimics the movement of lava in a lava lamp.
7. To keep the "lava lamp" going, simply add more Alka-Seltzer pieces as needed.

 EXPLANATION:

This experiment demonstrates the principles of density and immiscibility. Water and oil do not mix because they have different densities; water is denser than oil. The Alka-Seltzer tablet reacts with the water to release carbon dioxide gas, creating bubbles that rise through the less dense oil. As the gas escapes, the blobs of colored water sink back down, creating the mesmerizing lava lamp effect.

The Homemade Lava Lamp experiment is a captivating way to explore concepts of density, immiscibility, and chemical reactions. It's not only educational but also visually intriguing and perfect for sparking curiosity in young readers.

Include safety reminders, such as handling the Alka-Seltzer tablet with care and ensuring that the bottle is securely capped to prevent spills.

Invisible Ink Secrets

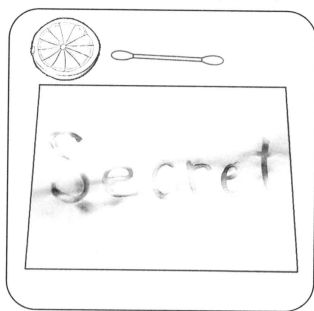

 **OBJECTIVE**

To create invisible ink and reveal hidden messages, introducing the concept of chemical reactions.

MATERIALS NEEDED:

- Lemon juice
- A small bowl or container
- White paper
- A paintbrush or cotton swab
- A heat source (e.g., a light bulb or an iron)

PROCEDURE:

1. Squeeze some lemon juice into a small bowl or container. Lemon juice contains citric acid, which will serve as your invisible ink.
2. Dip a paintbrush or cotton swab into the lemon juice.
3. Use the lemon juice-dipped brush or swab to write a secret message or draw a picture on a piece of white paper. Allow the paper to dry completely.
4. Once the lemon juice is dry, your message will be invisible to the naked eye.
5. To reveal the hidden message, gently heat the paper using a light bulb or an iron set on a low heat setting. Be sure to have adult supervision for this step if necessary.
6. As you heat the paper, the lemon juice will undergo a chemical reaction and turn brown, making your secret message visible.

 EXPLANATION:

This experiment demonstrates the concept of chemical reactions. The lemon juice, when applied to paper, is initially invisible because it's a weak acid. However, when exposed to heat, the acid reacts with the paper and oxidizes, turning brown and revealing your hidden message.

The Invisible Ink Secrets experiment is not only fun but also educational. It introduces young readers to the idea that some substances can undergo chemical changes under certain conditions, resulting in visible transformations.

Include safety precautions, such as adult supervision when using heat sources, and ensure that the heating process is done safely to avoid burns or accidents.

Time Travel Paradox

Imagine traveling back in time and meeting your younger self. Some scientists believe that time travel might be theoretically possible, but it's still a mystery with many paradoxes to unravel.

The Goldilocks Zone

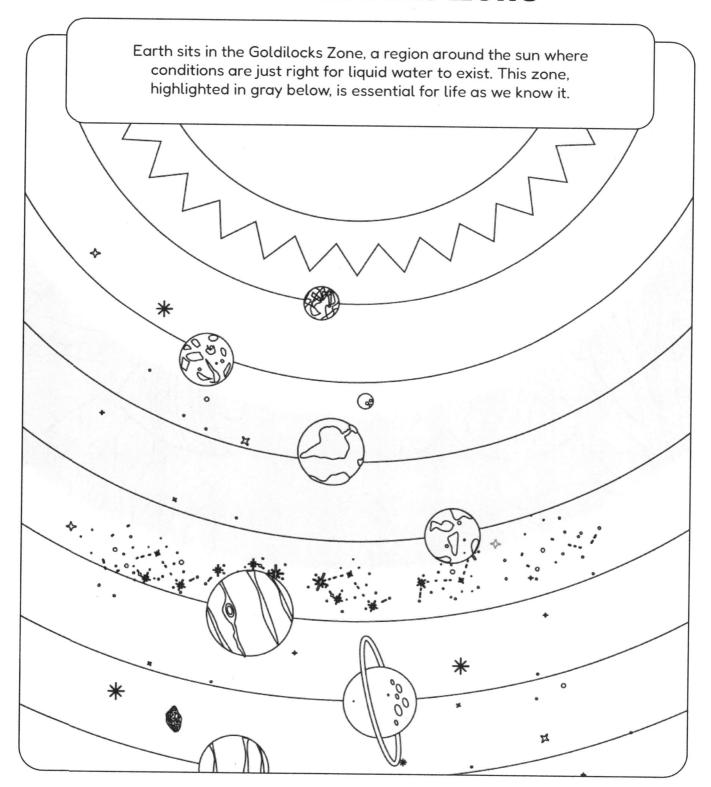

Earth sits in the Goldilocks Zone, a region around the sun where conditions are just right for liquid water to exist. This zone, highlighted in gray below, is essential for life as we know it.

The Largest Living Structure

The Great Barrier Reef in Australia is so enormous that it can be seen from space! It's the largest living structure on Earth and home to a dazzling array of marine life.

The Speed of Light

Light travels at an incredible speed of about 186,282 miles per second (299,792 kilometers per second). That's why we see things almost instantly when we flip a light switch.

Our Moon's Oddity

The moon is slowly moving away from Earth at a rate of about 1.5 inches (3.8 centimeters) per year. Billions of years ago, it was much closer, causing tides to be even more extreme.

The Scale of Atoms

Atoms, the building blocks of matter, are incredibly small.
If you lined up 100 million hydrogen atoms in a row, they would be
only about 1 centimeter long.

The World's Deepest Point

The Mariana Trench in the Pacific Ocean is the deepest part of the ocean, plunging to depths of about 36,070 feet (10,994 meters). That's deeper than Mount Everest is tall!

The Mighty Hummingbird

Hummingbirds are not only incredibly agile but also incredibly fast. Some species can beat their wings up to 80 times per second and reach speeds of 60 miles per hour (96.5 kilometers per hour).

The Internet's Weight

Did you know that the entire internet, including all the data and information stored on servers worldwide, weighs about the same as a strawberry?

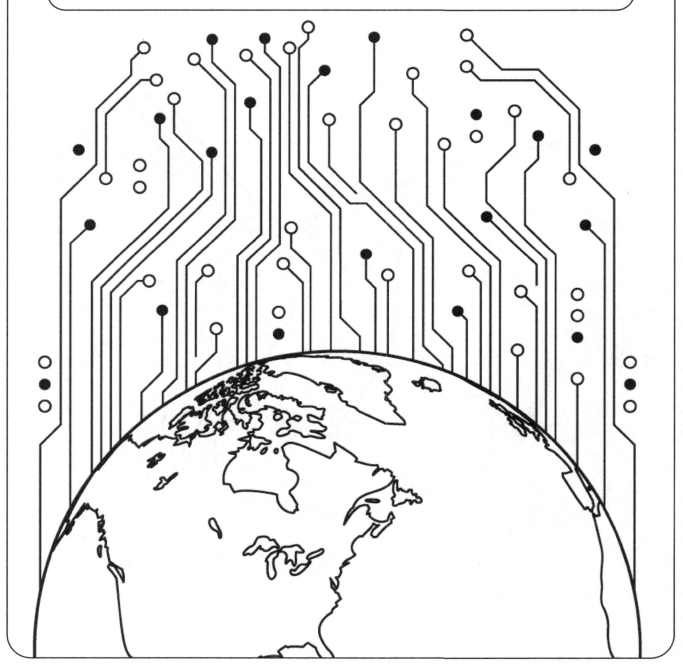

The Power of Lightning

A single bolt of lightning can heat the air around it to temperatures five times hotter than the surface of the sun! It's a dazzling display of nature's electricity.

Towering Mountains

Behold the majesty of Earth's mightiest peaks. These giants have been shaped by the forces of time, weather, and geological processes. From the rugged Himalayas to the majestic Andes, mountains stand as both a testament to Earth's power and a sanctuary for diverse ecosystems. Discover the wonders of mountain landscapes and the stories they tell about our planet's history.

Majestic Peaks

Explore the world's tallest and most iconic mountains, each with its unique charm and geological significance. From the grandeur of Mount Everest to the mystique of the Matterhorn, these peaks have beckoned adventurers and climbers for generations. Learn about the geological processes that formed these giants and the awe-inspiring stories of those who scaled their summits.

Pristine Lakes

Enter the realm of crystal-clear lakes, where tranquil waters mirror the surrounding beauty of nature. Lakes play a vital role in our planet's ecosystems, providing homes to diverse aquatic life and offering serene havens for those seeking tranquility. Learn about the significance of lakes, their formation, and the delicate balance they maintain within Earth's ecosystems.

Lakes: Jewels of the Earth

Journey to some of the world's most breathtaking lakes, from the sapphire-blue depths of Lake Baikal to the enchanting landscapes of Plitvice Lakes National Park. Explore the unique features that make each lake a natural wonder, from the world's deepest to the mesmerizing colors of their waters. Delve into the importance of conservation to protect these aquatic gems.

Cascading Waterfalls

Witness the sheer power and beauty of waterfalls, where nature's force is on full display. Waterfalls captivate with their dynamic energy and stunning visuals. Learn about the geological processes that create these natural wonders and the significant role they play in shaping our landscapes.

The World's Most Spectacular Waterfalls

Embark on a journey to the world's most iconic waterfalls, from the thundering majesty of Niagara Falls to the ethereal beauty of Angel Falls. Discover the science behind their formation and the awe they inspire in visitors. Explore the cultural significance and stories surrounding these cascading wonders.

Mystical Caves

Descend into the hidden world of caves, where Earth's secrets lie beneath the surface. Caves have been formed over millions of years by geological processes, and they harbor unique ecosystems and stunning formations. Explore the enchanting underground realms and the science behind cave formation.

Caves Explored

Delve into the exploration of caves, from the exploration of vast underground chambers to the discovery of delicate stalactites and stalagmites. Learn about the techniques and equipment used by cave explorers, and discover the significance of cave conservation to protect these subterranean wonders.

Dance of the Northern Lights

Beneath the starry northern skies, a celestial spectacle unfolds—the Northern Lights, or aurora borealis. These enchanting lights paint the night with vibrant colors, captivating observers with their mystical dance. But what causes this breathtaking phenomenon? Let's delve into the science and magic of the Northern Lights.

The Aurora Borealis: Nature's Light Show

The Aurora Borealis, or Northern Lights, occurs when charged particles from the sun interact with the Earth's magnetosphere, causing ionization and emission of light in the polar regions. These mesmerizing displays result from the collision of these charged particles with atmospheric gases, producing vibrant hues of green, pink, and purple in the night sky.

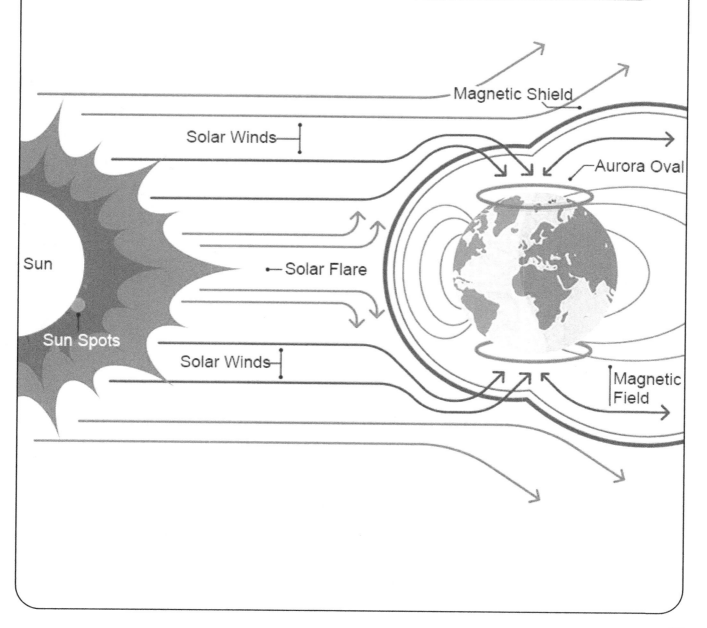

Fury of Thunderstorms

Thunderstorms unleash the fury of nature in electrifying displays of lightning, thunder, and rain. These atmospheric juggernauts are both captivating and formidable. Join us as we explore the inner workings of thunderstorms and the awe they inspire.

Anatomy of a Thunderstorm

Thunderstorms form when warm, moist air rises, creating cumulonimbus clouds. Electrical charges within these clouds result in lightning and thunder. The storms bring rain, hail, and strong winds, making them dynamic meteorological events.

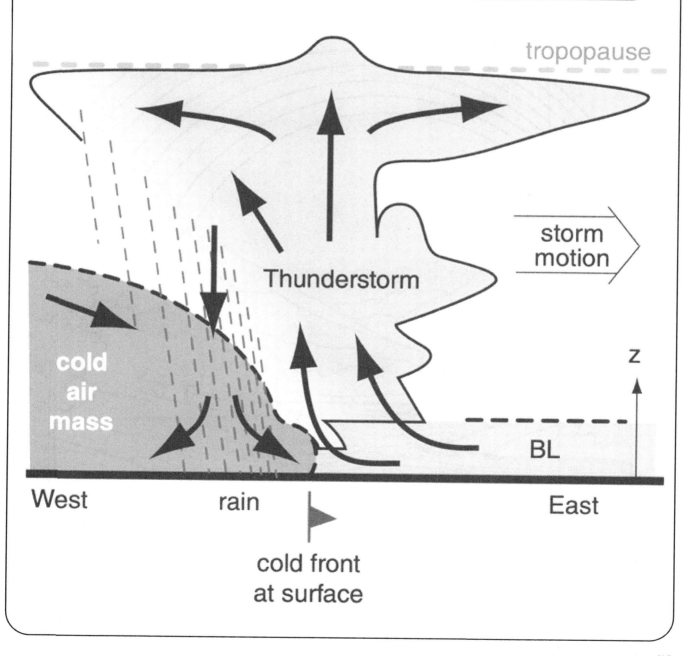

The Delicate Dance of Rainbows

Rainbows, with their graceful arcs of color, have fascinated humanity for centuries. These optical marvels appear after rain showers, painting the sky with vivid hues. Explore the physics and wonder of rainbows and the folklore that surrounds them.

Rainbows: Nature's Prism

Rainbows occur when sunlight refracts, reflects, and disperses in raindrops, creating a spectrum of colors in the sky. As sunlight enters a raindrop, it bends, reflecting off the inner surface and separating into its constituent colors.

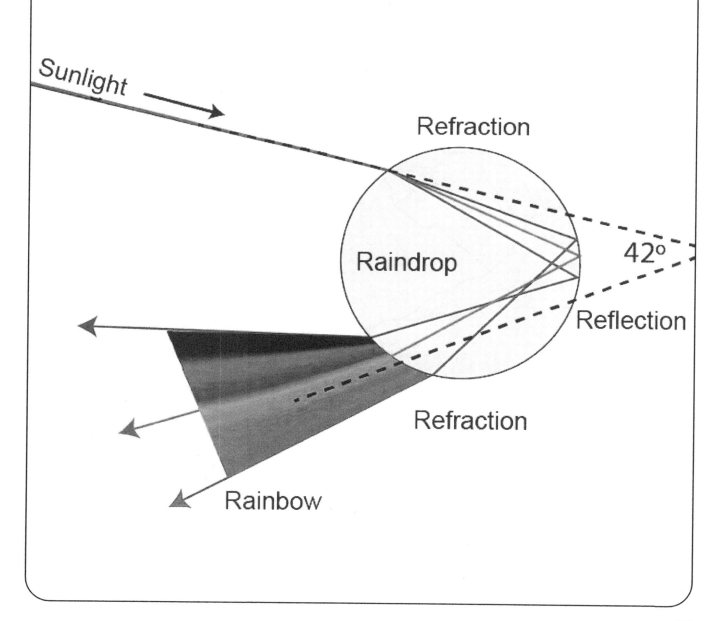

Weather Wonders Explored

As we conclude our journey through the world of weather wonders, we invite you to explore further. From auroras to thunderstorms to rainbows, Earth's atmosphere offers a tapestry of awe-inspiring phenomena. Join us in unraveling the mysteries and appreciating the beauty of our ever-changing skies.

Coral Reefs: Underwater Worlds

Beneath the glistening surface of our oceans lies a world of wonder—coral reefs. These vibrant and diverse ecosystems are not only breathtaking but also vital for marine life. Let's dive into the mesmerizing world of coral reefs and unveil their significance in our planet's underwater tapestry.

The Secret Life of Coral Reefs

Join us on a journey beneath the waves to explore the hidden treasures of coral reefs. Through captivating images, we'll witness the kaleidoscope of colors, intricate coral formations, and the bustling marine communities that call these reefs home. Discover the science behind coral reef formation, the threats they face, and the efforts to protect them.

The Serengeti: Africa's Wild Heart

Venture into the heart of Africa, where the sweeping savannas of the Serengeti stretch as far as the eye can see. This iconic ecosystem pulses with life, featuring an array of wildlife and extraordinary landscapes. Explore the intricate web of interactions that make the Serengeti a true marvel of nature.

Serengeti: Symphony of the Wild

Immerse yourself in the world of the Serengeti through striking images of its charismatic inhabitants. From the thundering herds of wildebeests to the regal lions and elusive leopards, discover the captivating stories of survival and adaptation. Learn about the conservation efforts aimed at preserving this African treasure.

Amazon Rainforest: Lungs of the Earth

Enter the world's largest tropical rainforest—the Amazon. This vast expanse of greenery is not only a haven for biodiversity but also plays a critical role in maintaining Earth's climate. Explore the awe-inspiring beauty and ecological importance of the Amazon rainforest.

The Amazon's Green Treasure

Embark on an expedition into the heart of the Amazon rainforest, where lush vegetation teems with life. Through captivating images, encounter unique wildlife, ancient tribes, and the rich biodiversity of this remarkable ecosystem. Learn about the Amazon's vital role in carbon storage, its challenges, and the efforts to safeguard its future.

Ecosystems in Harmony Explored

As we conclude our journey through Ecosystems in Harmony, we invite you to explore the interconnectedness of Earth's diverse environments. From coral reefs to savannas to rainforests, our planet's ecosystems are a testament to the delicate balance of life. Join us in celebrating the remarkable harmony of nature.

Hidden Caves and Underground Marvels

Beneath the Earth's surface lies a labyrinth of hidden wonders waiting to be discovered. Caves, caverns, and underground rivers weave a mysterious tapestry that intrigues explorers and scientists alike. Join us as we descend into the depths to unveil the geological treasures hidden below.

Journey into Earth's Depths

Embark on a subterranean adventure through stunning images and narratives. Explore the intricate formations of caves, the flowing beauty of underground rivers, and the marvels of underground ecosystems. Learn about the geological processes that shape these hidden realms and the awe they inspire in those who venture within.

Lost Worlds:
Ancient Civilizations and Their Secrets

The remnants of ancient civilizations hold the keys to unlocking the mysteries of human history. Buried beneath layers of time, their cities, artifacts, and enigmatic symbols offer tantalizing glimpses into bygone eras. Journey back in time as we unravel the enigmas of lost worlds.

Unearthing Ancient Mysteries

Delve into the world of archaeology and historical discovery through evocative images and stories. Explore the ruins of ancient cities, decipher the writings of forgotten civilizations, and ponder the riddles left behind by our ancestors. Join us in uncovering the secrets that still lie dormant in the sands of time.

Unexplained Phenomena: Earth's Puzzling Enigmas

Earth is no stranger to the unexplained. Mysterious phenomena, from crop circles to geological anomalies to UFOs, challenge our understanding of the world around us. In this section, we confront the perplexing and delve into the world of Earth's most enigmatic puzzles.

Unraveling Earth's Enigmas

Peer into the world of the unexplained through striking visuals and accounts of baffling events. Encounter the bewildering occurrences that have confounded scientists and skeptics, from inexplicable lights in the sky to bizarre geological formations. Explore the various theories and investigations aimed at unraveling these enduring mysteries.

The Ocean's Depths: Secrets of the Deep Blue

Beneath the surface of the ocean lies a realm of darkness and mystery. The deep-sea abyss conceals creatures and landscapes that defy imagination. Join us as we plunge into the depths of the ocean to explore the wonders hidden in the inky blue.

Exploring the Abyss

Embark on an underwater odyssey through mesmerizing imagery and tales of deep-sea exploration. Encounter the bizarre and alien-like creatures that inhabit the ocean's depths, discover shipwrecks and submerged landscapes, and learn about the challenges faced by intrepid scientists who venture into this mysterious world.

Natural Wonders of the World

Our planet is adorned with breathtaking natural formations that defy imagination. From cascading waterfalls to towering mountain ranges, these wonders of nature leave us spellbound. Join us as we journey to some of the most spectacular landscapes on Earth.

Marvels Carved by Nature

In-depth exploration of natural wonders awaits. Traverse through high-quality images and descriptions of these natural marvels. Witness the raw power of geological forces and the timeless beauty they have sculpted over eons. Learn about the formation and significance of these awe-inspiring landmarks.

Architectural Marvels

Humans have harnessed their creativity and engineering prowess to build architectural wonders that defy gravity and imagination. From towering skyscrapers to historical monuments, these structures are a testament to human achievement. Join us on a journey through iconic landmarks.

The World's Architectural Wonders

Unveil the architectural masterpieces that grace our cities and landscapes. Architectural drawings and photographs showcase the brilliance of design and engineering. Delve into the history, significance, and cultural impact of these remarkable structures.

Cultural and Historical Landmarks

Through centuries, humans have erected landmarks that bear witness to their history, culture, and heritage. Temples, palaces, and UNESCO World Heritage Sites transport us to bygone eras. Explore the world's cultural tapestry through these extraordinary landmarks.

Legacy of the Past: Cultural Landmarks

Immerse yourself in the historical richness and cultural significance of these landmarks. Stunning images capture the beauty and architecture of these sites. Stories and anecdotes provide insights into the historical context and preservation efforts that safeguard our shared heritage.

Landmarks of Environmental Importance

Earth's natural beauty and ecological significance are celebrated through landmarks like national parks and conservation areas. These protected spaces are essential for preserving biodiversity and ecosystems. Join us in discovering the vital role they play in safeguarding our planet's health.

Preserving Our Natural Heritage

Embark on a journey through pristine landscapes teeming with biodiversity. Photographs showcase the natural wonders and scenic beauty of protected areas. Learn about the crucial conservation efforts and the importance of preserving these ecological treasures for future generations.

Natural Wonders of the World

In this part, we embark on a journey to explore the breathtaking natural wonders that adorn our planet. From cascading waterfalls to towering mountains, these illustrations transport you to some of Earth's most remarkable landscapes.

Waterfall Majesty

Marvel at the artistic renderings of magnificent waterfalls from around the world. Each illustration brings to life the power and grace of these cascading wonders, from the iconic Victoria Falls to the serene Angel Falls.

Mountain Grandeur

Scale the heights of artistic interpretation as you explore illustrations of majestic mountain ranges. These illustrations capture the grandeur of peaks like the Himalayas and the Andes, inviting you to embark on a visual expedition.

Desert Landscapes

Delve into the artistic depiction of diverse desert landscapes, from the endless dunes of the Sahara to the otherworldly beauty of Arizona's Antelope Canyon. These illustrations reveal the stark and mesmerizing allure of arid terrains.

Verdant Forests

Experience the vibrant greenery of Earth's lush forests through these illustrations. From the Amazon Rainforest to the temperate woodlands of Europe, these depictions celebrate the biodiversity and tranquility of wooded landscapes.

Architectural Icons

Enter the realm of human ingenuity and creativity with these artistic representations of architectural marvels. From iconic skyscrapers to historical monuments, these illustrations capture the essence of human achievement.

Cultural Heritage

Travel through time and culture as you explore illustrations of culturally significant landmarks. From ancient temples to opulent palaces, these depictions offer a glimpse into the rich tapestry of human history and heritage.

Ecological Treasures

Journey to the world's most precious natural areas through these illustrations. From protected national parks to pristine marine sanctuaries, these depictions showcase the ecological treasures that must be preserved for future generations.

The Microscopic Realm

As we peer through powerful microscopes, we are introduced to a realm where life takes on new dimensions. In these illustrations, we unveil the hidden worlds of microorganisms, cells, and molecules. Explore the complexity and diversity of life that thrives beyond our ordinary perception and witness the beauty of the tiny universe.

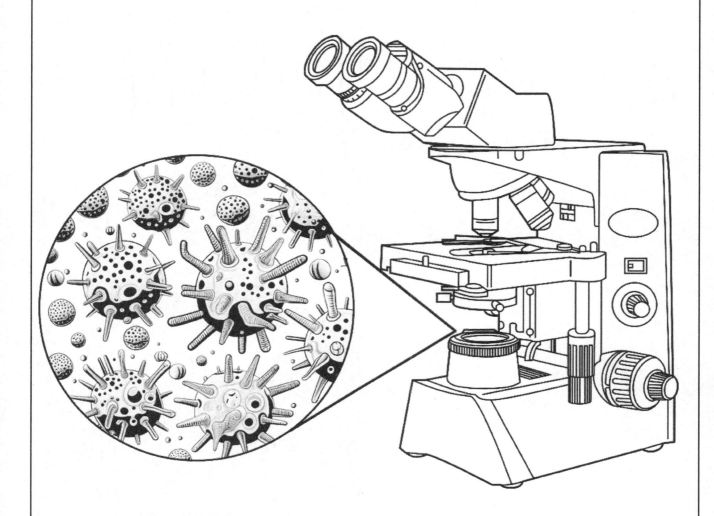

This illustration showcases the rich biodiversity of the microscopic realm, emphasizing the countless life forms that exist beyond our sight.

MICROSCOPIC MARVELS

Explore the inner workings of a eukaryotic cell, where various organelles
collaborate to maintain life's essential functions

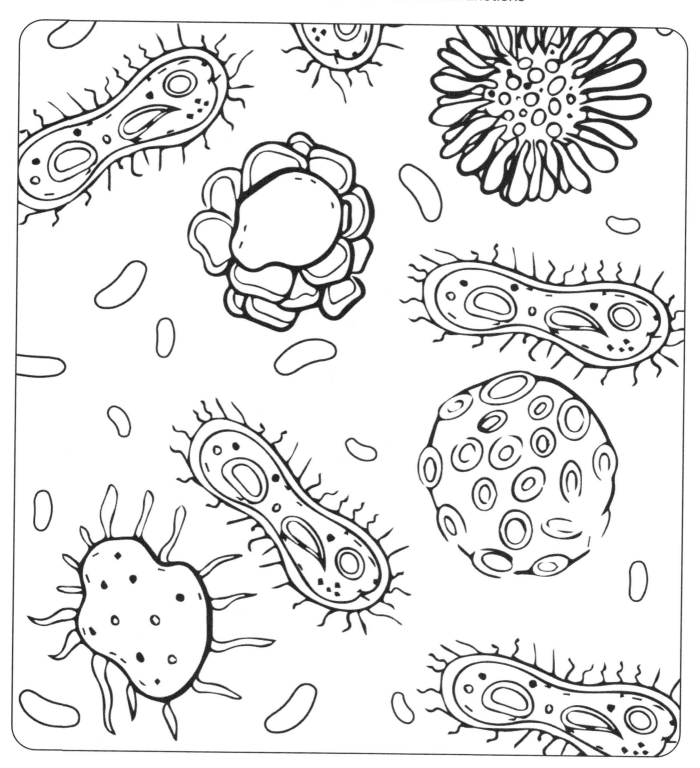

Cellular Machinery

Within the microscopic world, the machinery of life operates with astounding precision. These illustrations delve deep into the cellular structures and organelles that make life possible. Discover how cells function as intricate factories, carrying out processes essential for all living organisms.

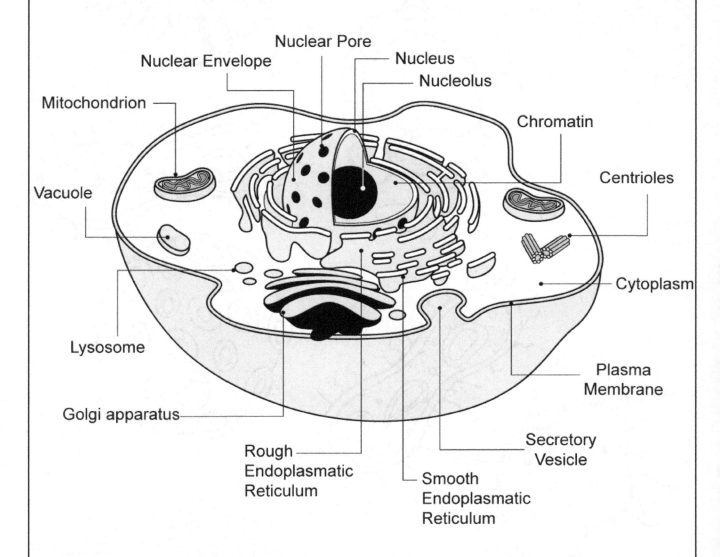

Nuclear Pore
Nuclear Envelope
Nucleus
Nucleolus
Mitochondrion
Chromatin
Centrioles
Vacuole
Cytoplasm
Lysosome
Plasma Membrane
Golgi apparatus
Secretory Vesicle
Rough Endoplasmatic Reticulum
Smooth Endoplasmatic Reticulum

This illustration delves into the a cell's structure and function, showcasing different parts that have crucial roles in energy production.

MICROSCOPIC MARVELS

The human body consists of a diverse array of cells, ranging from brain cells, liver cells, blood cells, muscle cells, instestinal cells, and more.

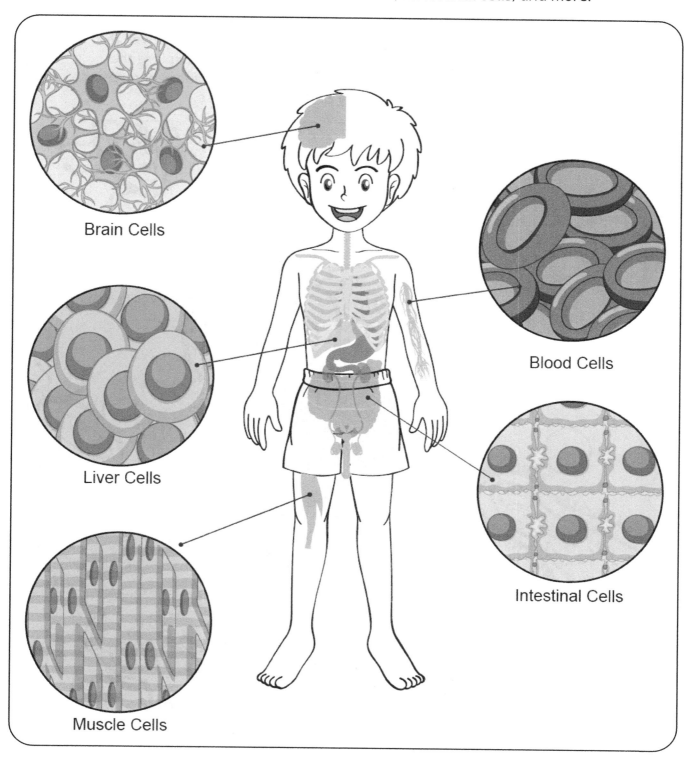

Brain Cells

Liver Cells

Muscle Cells

Blood Cells

Intestinal Cells

The Microscopic Realm

As we peer through powerful microscopes, we are introduced to a realm where life takes on new dimensions. In these illustrations, we unveil the hidden worlds of microorganisms, cells, and molecules. Explore the complexity and diversity of life that thrives beyond our ordinary perception and witness the beauty of the tiny universe.

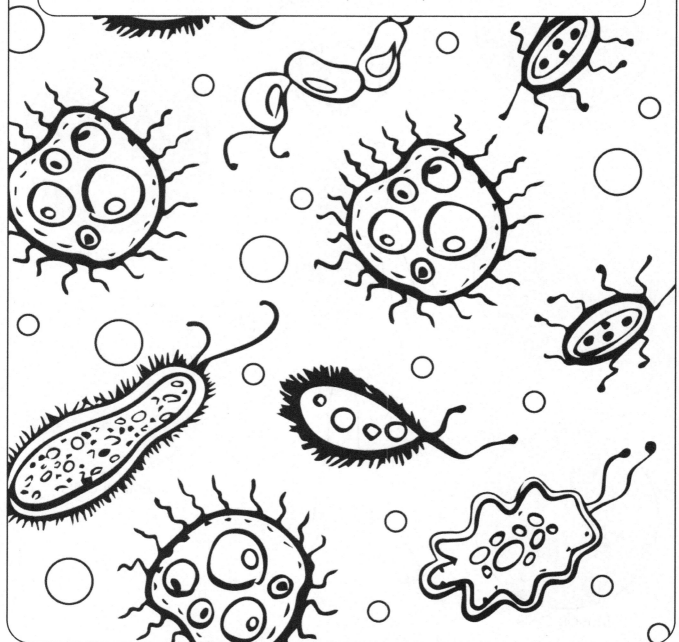

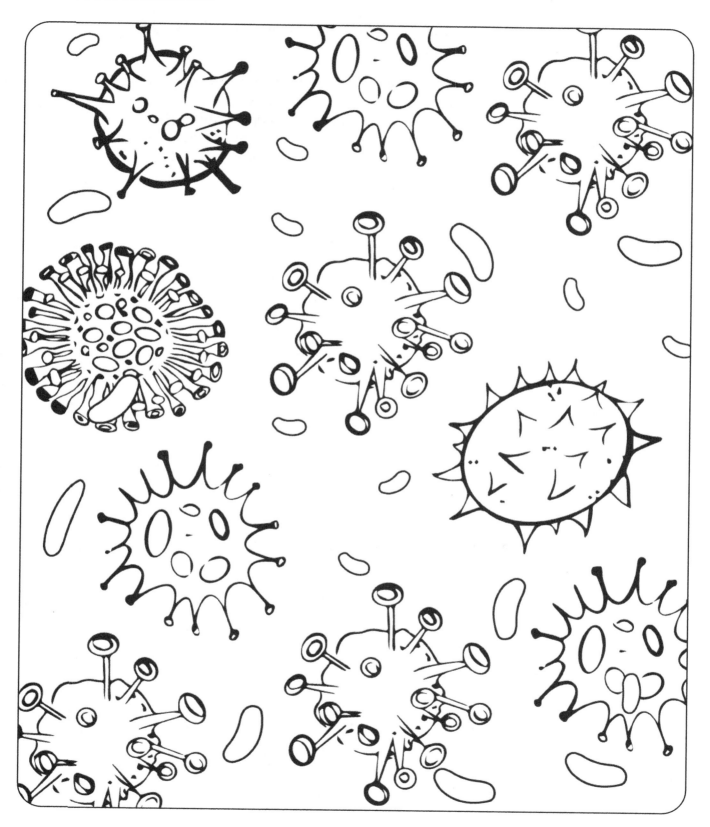

Nanotechnology Marvels

Nanotechnology, a field at the forefront of science and engineering, explores the manipulation of matter at the nanoscale. In these illustrations, we marvel at nanoscale devices, materials, and applications that have revolutionized various industries. Witness the incredible potential of nanotechnology in medicine, electronics, and beyond.

MICROSCOPIC MARVELS

Nanotechnology is used in transforming medicine by enabling precise drug delivery and diagnostics at the nanoscale.

Microbial Diversity

Prepare to journey into a realm where diversity knows no bounds. In these illustrations, we unveil the myriad faces of microorganisms. From bacteria and archaea to microeukaryotes, each presents its own unique charm. Explore the astonishing variety of microorganisms and their profound impact on Earth's ecosystems.

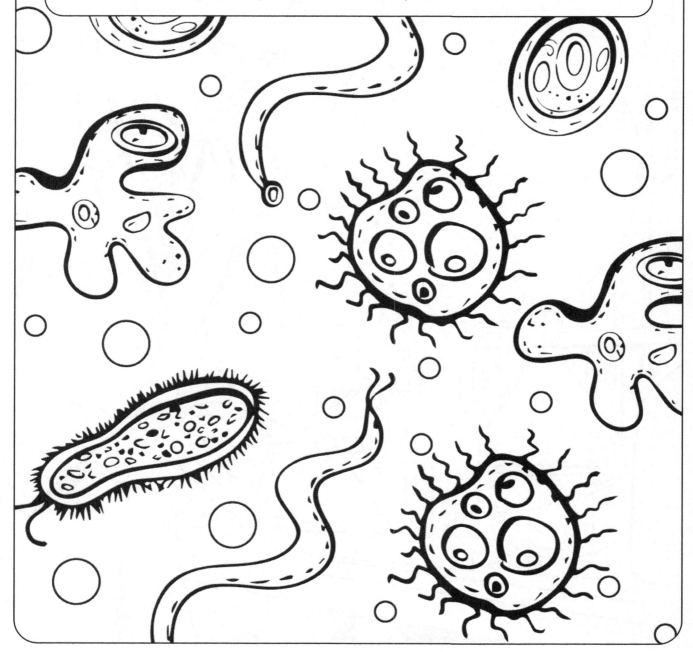

MICROORGANISMS AND BEYOND

Explore the captivating world of bacterial diversity, where each bacterium is a testament to the endless forms microorganisms can take.

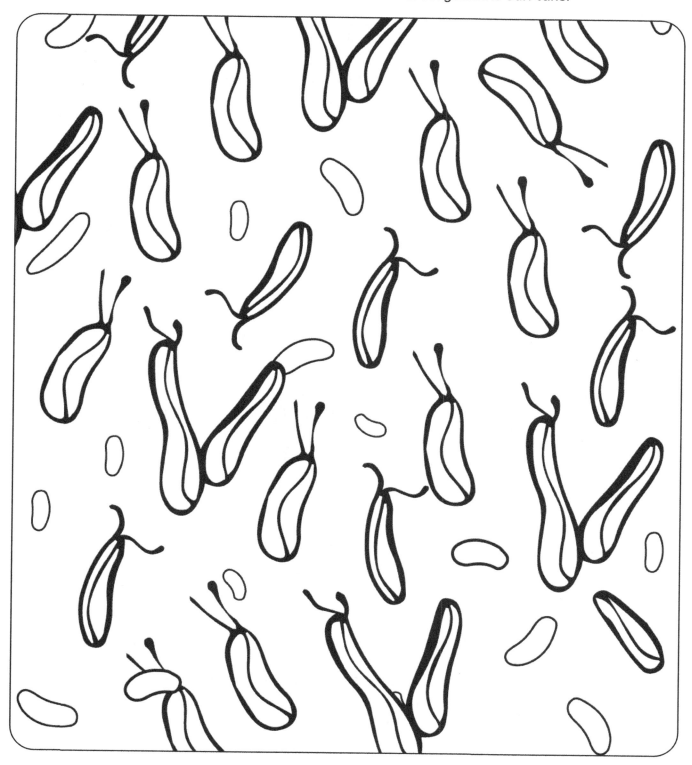

Microbes and Human Health

Within the microscopic world, microorganisms play a dual role as both friend and foe. These illustrations illuminate the complex relationship between microbes and the human body. Discover the intricate dance of beneficial microbes and potential pathogens, and gain insight into their pivotal roles in human health.

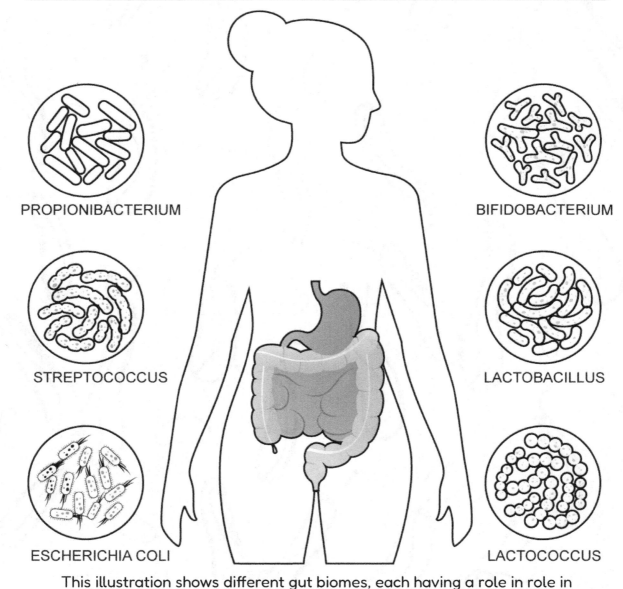

PROPIONIBACTERIUM

BIFIDOBACTERIUM

STREPTOCOCCUS

LACTOBACILLUS

ESCHERICHIA COLI

LACTOCOCCUS

This illustration shows different gut biomes, each having a role in role in digestive well-being.

MICROORGANISMS AND BEYOND

Human pathogens are microscopic invaders, such as bacteria and viruses, that can cause illnesses by disrupting the body's normal functions and triggering immune responses.

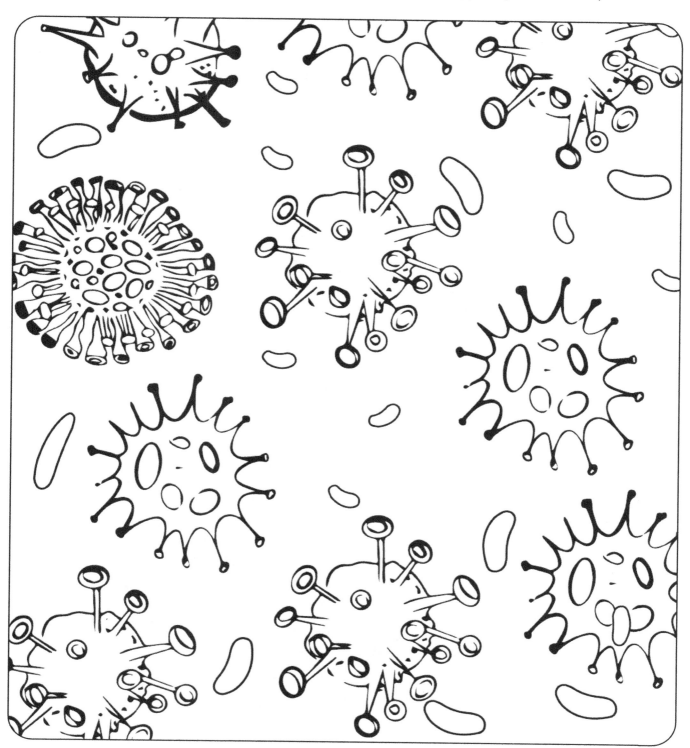

Microbes in Ecosystems

Microorganisms are the unsung heroes of Earth's ecosystems. In these artistic depictions, we delve into the essential roles played by microorganisms in ecological processes. Witness the microscopic architects responsible for nutrient cycling, decomposition, and the maintenance of environmental balance.

Extremophiles and Astrobiology

Life thrives in the most unexpected places, even beyond Earth's boundaries. These illustrations introduce you to extremophiles—microorganisms that defy extreme conditions. Explore how these extremophiles expand our understanding of life's possibilities, making them key players in the field of astrobiology.

MICROORGANISMS AND BEYOND

Tardigrades, also known as water bears, are tiny, resilient creatures capable of surviving extreme conditions, including high radiation, intense heat, and the vacuum of space.

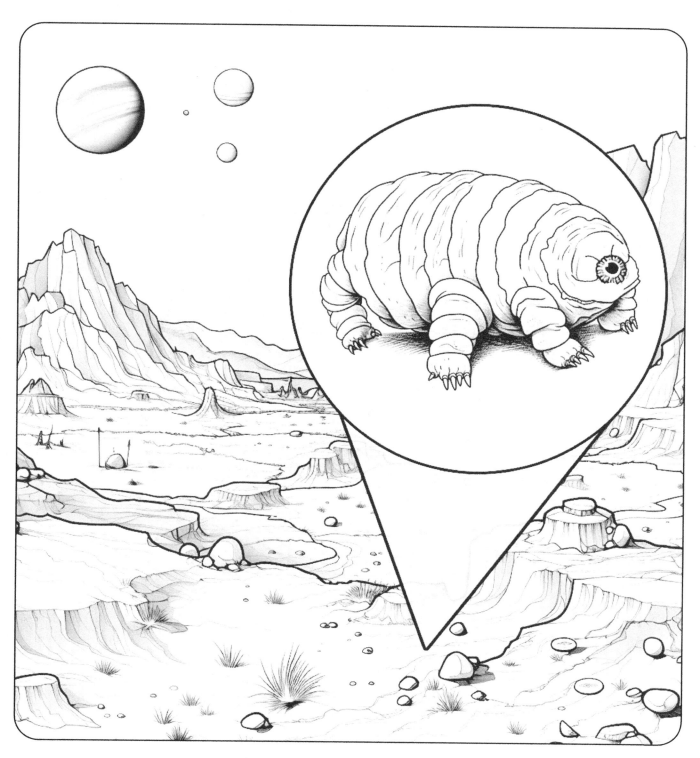

Solar System Surprises

Our journey into the cosmos begins with a closer look at our own celestial neighborhood—the Solar System. As we turn our gaze to the planets, moons, and the radiant Sun, we uncover a tapestry of astronomical marvels. Did you know that Venus experiences scorching temperatures due to a runaway greenhouse effect, or that Saturn boasts majestic rings composed of icy particles? Join us on a voyage through the Solar System and uncover the incredible facts that make each celestial body unique.

Venus, the second planet from the Sun, experiences scorching temperatures due to a runaway greenhouse effect.

SPACE FACTS

Saturn's stunning rings are a mesmerizing feature of our Solar System.
The illustration showcases their intricate beauty.

Galaxies: Beyond Our Imagination

Venturing deeper into the cosmos, we encounter galaxies—vast islands of stars, gas, and dust that stretch across the universe. The Milky Way, our cosmic home, is just one among billions of galaxies in the observable universe. Explore the sheer diversity of galaxies, from spirals adorned with graceful arms to irregular galaxies with chaotic forms. Peer into the heart of nebulae, the cosmic cradles of starbirth, and grasp the grandeur of the cosmos.

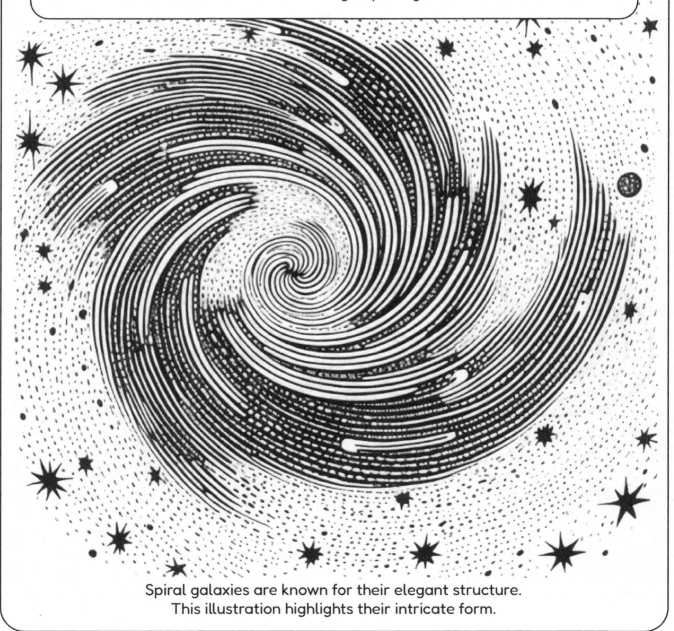

Spiral galaxies are known for their elegant structure.
This illustration highlights their intricate form.

Nebulae are the birthplaces of stars.
This illustration captures the cosmic nursery where stars come to life.

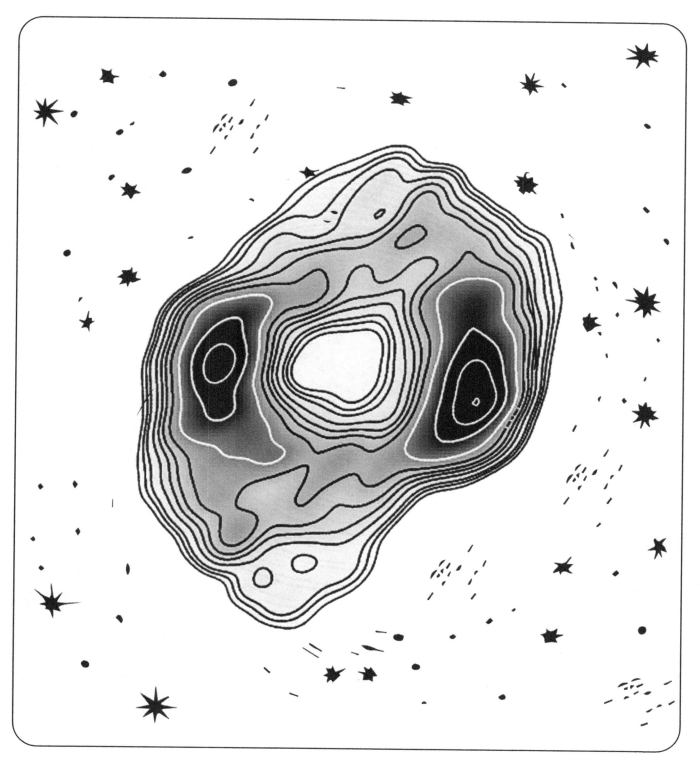

Cosmic Wonders and Anomalies

The universe is teeming with extraordinary phenomena and enigmatic anomalies that challenge our understanding of physics and astrophysics. Discover the awe-inspiring power of black holes, where gravity is so intense that nothing, not even light, can escape. Witness the explosive brilliance of supernovae, the cataclysmic deaths of massive stars. Dive into the mysteries of dark matter and dark energy, two invisible forces that shape the destiny of the cosmos.

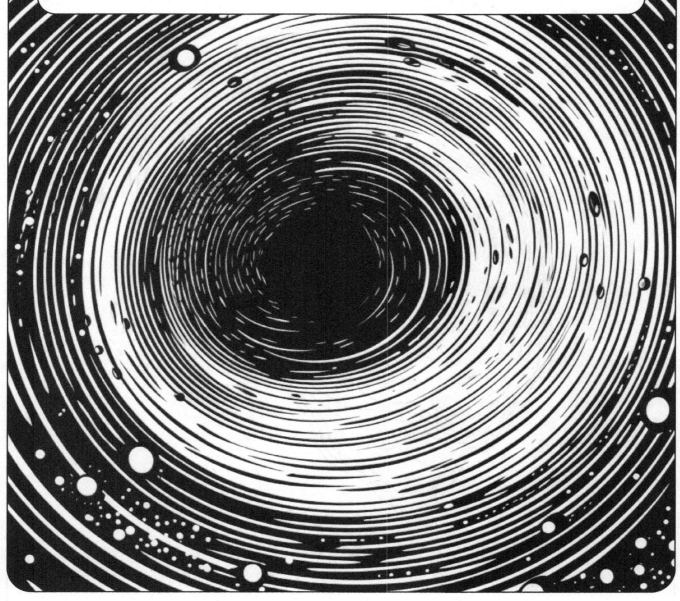

Black holes warp spacetime with their immense gravity.
This illustration conveys the concept of gravitational bending.

SPACE FACTS

Supernovae are some of the most energetic events in the universe.
This illustration depicts the explosive release of energy.

Human Reach into the Stars

Throughout history, humanity has reached for the stars with remarkable achievements in space exploration. From the first human steps on the Moon to the distant exploration of planets and asteroids, our quest for knowledge has taken us to incredible heights. Learn about the iconic missions, like Apollo 11, Voyager, and the Mars rovers, that have expanded our understanding of the cosmos and opened doors to further exploration.

The Apollo 11 mission marked a monumental achievement in human history. This illustration commemorates the historic Moon landing.

SPACE FACTS

Voyager probes have ventured into interstellar space.
This illustration showcases their path to the stars.

Life in Space: Challenges and Joys

As astronauts leave the safety of Earth, they enter a realm unlike any other—a world of microgravity, vacuum, and unparalleled beauty. In the vastness of space, astronauts carry out daily tasks that are both challenging and joyous. Witness them eating, working, and conducting experiments in the unique environment of a space station. Learn how they adapt to life without gravity and find moments of wonder in the cosmos.

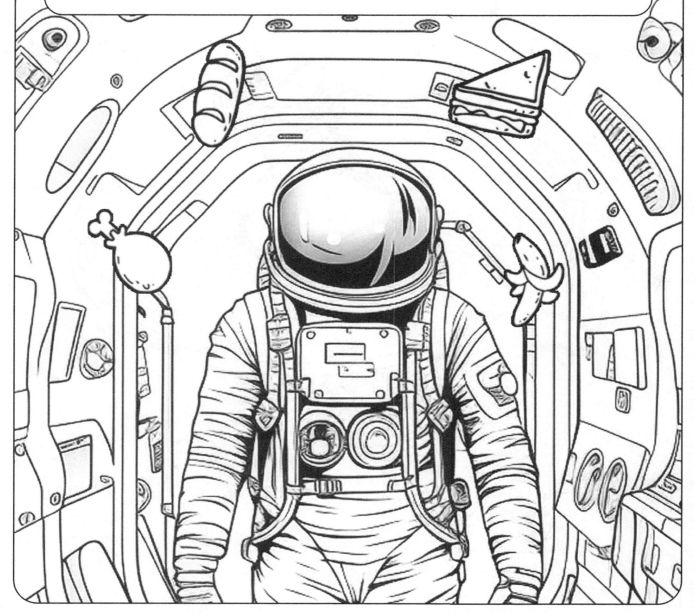

This illustration depicts the unique experience of astronauts dining in space, where food hovers before them in a weightless environment.

ASTRONAUT ADVENTURES

Astronauts perform a wide range of tasks in space, including vital scientific research. This illustration captures their dedication to advancing our understanding of the cosmos.

Spacewalks: Dancing in the Void

Imagine stepping out of the protective confines of a spacecraft into the abyss of space itself—a spacewalk. Astronauts don their spacesuits and embark on this ultimate adventure, floating in the void, repairing spacecraft, and conducting experiments. Experience the adrenaline rush and profound sense of freedom that comes with a spacewalk, where astronauts become cosmic dancers, gracefully maneuvering through the vacuum of space.

This illustration portrays the breathtaking adventure of a spacewalk, highlighting the astronaut's tethered float in the cosmic void.

ASTRONAUT ADVENTURES

Astronauts often perform critical maintenance and repairs during spacewalks.
This illustration captures the precision and skill required for these tasks.

Astronaut's View: Earth as a Jewel

Few experiences can match the breathtaking view of our planet from the window of a spacecraft. Astronauts have the privilege of seeing Earth as a radiant jewel against the backdrop of the cosmos. Explore artistic representations that capture this unique perspective. Witness the beauty of our blue planet, the ever-changing weather patterns, and the luminous cities at night, all from space.

This artistic representation captures the stunning beauty of Earth as seen from space, emphasizing its vibrant colors and the vastness of the cosmos beyond.

ASTRONAUT ADVENTURES

This illustration showcases the mesmerizing sight of cities lit up at night, offering a unique perspective on human civilization.

Challenges of Deep Space Exploration

The quest for knowledge and exploration extends beyond our immediate celestial neighborhood. Join astronauts as they venture to distant worlds, asteroids, and moons. Encounter the challenges they face in deep space exploration, from navigating through asteroid fields to landing on alien landscapes. Discover the rewards of expanding our horizons and uncovering the secrets of the cosmos.

This illustration portrays the excitement of exploring distant worlds and the challenges astronauts face in navigating and conducting research on alien terrain.

ASTRONAUT ADVENTURES

Deep space exploration often involves navigating through treacherous asteroid fields. This illustration conveys the intensity of such missions.

Cosmic Landscapes

As we gaze into the night sky, we are often drawn to the breathtaking beauty of distant galaxies, meteor shower, and asteroids. Artists have the power to transform scientific data into stunning visual representations. Here, we present artistic interpretations of cosmic landscapes that transport us to the far reaches of the universe.

A meteor shower is a celestial event where multiple meteors streak across the night sky, originating from the Earth's passage through the debris left by a comet, creating a captivating and luminous display.

SPACE ILLUSTRATIONS

Asteroids are rocky and metallic objects that orbit the Sun,
mainly found in the asteroid belt between Mars and Jupiter.

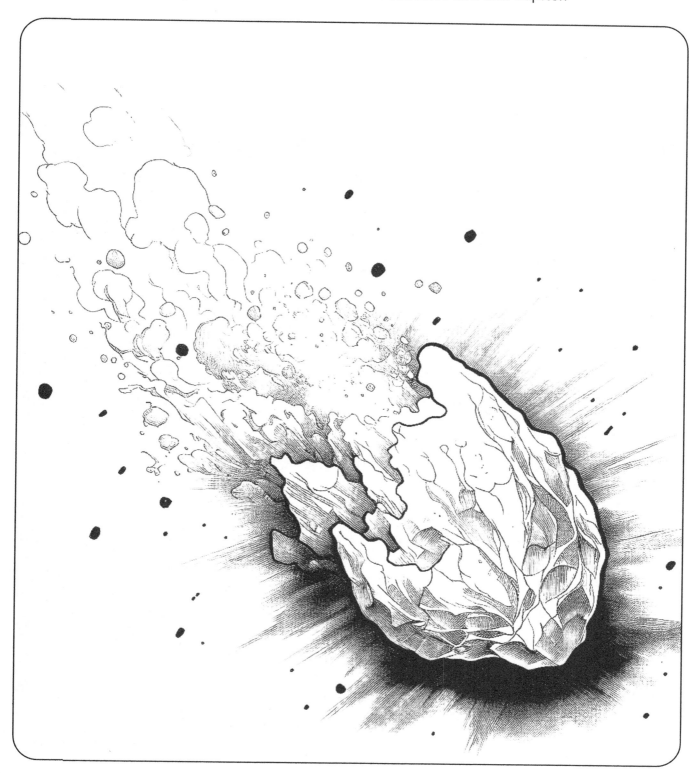

Astronomical Phenomena

The universe is filled with awe-inspiring astronomical phenomena, from the explosive brilliance of supernovae to the mysterious depths of black holes. These illustrations capture the essence of these cosmic marvels, allowing us to appreciate the science and beauty behind them. Journey through the cosmos and witness the extraordinary events that shape our understanding of the universe.

Constellations are patterns of stars that form recognizable shapes or figures in the night sky.

SPACE ILLUSTRATIONS

Comets are icy bodies in space, characterized by glowing tails when they approach the sun.

Space Exploration

Humanity's quest to explore the cosmos has led to remarkable achievements in space exploration. These illustrations bring to life the spacecraft, rovers, and astronauts who venture into the great unknown. Experience the excitement and challenges of space missions as you peer into the imaginative world of space exploration.

The illustration showcases a robotic explorer on Mars, conducting scientific experiments and traversing the Martian surface.

SPACE ILLUSTRATIONS

This illustration captures the breathtaking experience of an astronaut on a spacewalk, high above our planet.

Exoplanets and Alien Worlds

The discovery of exoplanets—worlds orbiting distant stars—opens a window to the possibility of alien landscapes and the search for extraterrestrial life. These illustrations transport us to these far-off realms, allowing us to envision the landscapes and environments of exoplanets in distant star systems. Let your imagination roam as you contemplate the mysteries of these distant worlds.

Explore an artist's vision of an exoplanet's surface, sparking curiosity about the possibilities of extraterrestrial landscapes.

SPACE ILLUSTRATIONS

This illustration invites readers to contemplate the diverse atmospheres and weather patterns of exoplanets.

Made in the USA
Las Vegas, NV
02 December 2024

13213215R00066